An Ignatian Approach to Reading the Old Testament

John Goldingay

David Allan Hubbard Professor of Old Testament
Fuller Theological Seminary, Pasadena, California

GW00657884

GROVE BOOKS LIMITED
RIDLEY HALL RD CAMBRIDGE CB3 9HU

Contents

Preface

I am grateful to Doug Gregg (who first invited me to join a group to follow the Ignatian Exercises), Catherine Gregg, David Thornton, Janice Strength, Roberta King, and Ann Goldingay (the mute presence at our groups) for many elements in what follows. Together we first worked through the Exercises on the Life of Christ, profited profoundly from them, sensed the need for a more accessible version especially for people for whom the elements that reflected Ignatius' medieval Catholicism were an obstacle, agreed further on the need for an Old Testament equivalent, and test-drove a draft of one. You can find a version of a New Testament reading scheme along the lines of the Old Testament one, with readings for thirty weeks, at www.fuller.edu/theology/faculty/goldingay. I will also post there any comments on the contents of this booklet that I think might interest people.

If you use either of the reading schemes and have comments that would help in revising them, please write to me at JohnGold@Fuller.edu. If you want to obtain this booklet in the USA, you can order it from the Grove website www.grovebooks.co.uk or send a check for $4 per copy including postage to me at 111 South Orange Grove Boulevard, #108, Pasadena, CA, 91105.

The Cover Illustration is by Peter Ashton

Copyright © John Goldingay 2002

First Impression June 2002
ISSN 1365-490X
ISBN 1 85174 501 7

Ignatius and the Nature of Biblical Interpretation 1

Ignatius of Loyola was born in 1491, a contemporary of Luther and Calvin. He was a Spanish soldier of aristocratic background, a Christian with the usual enthusiasm of a young man for life and love.

Recuperating at home after being wounded in battle at thirty, through reading the life of Christ and reflecting on his own life he came to a dramatic realization of its pointlessness. It led him to reshape his life and dedicate it to God as a monk. He then found himself involved in encouraging spiritual growth among both lay people and monks. The 'Exercises' on the life of Christ that he thus developed were designed to encourage people to reflect on what their lives were about and where God might be directing them. There are many editions of the Exercises; the one I chiefly use is *The Spiritual Exercises of St Ignatius* translated by Anthony Mottola, with an introduction by Robert W Gleason (reprinted New York: Doubleday, 1989). Ignatian spirituality is thus much more than merely a way of reading the Bible, but our focus here is on that aspect of its significance.

> *The 'Exercises' were designed to encourage people to reflect on what their lives were about*

G W F Hegel suggested a three-stage model for understanding the history of thought. Some theory or thesis is accepted. Then, a counter-thesis or antithesis gains acceptance. Third, a synthesis combines the truths in the first two. Current conventional wisdom implies a Hegelian understanding of the history of biblical interpretation. In the first millennium there was pre-modern interpretation, the second millennium saw the development of modern interpretation, and in the third there is postmodern interpretation. Calling this 'the conventional wisdom' implies a recognition that it may look silly in a few years time. Associating it with Hegel implies a recognition that it imposes categories on the history and reflects our need to understand matters in a way that provides them with some structure and provides history with closure. But it is still a helpful framework.

Pre-modern interpretation is conveniently illustrated for us by the New Testament's interpretation of the Old Testament, which for the early Christians was simply the Scriptures. These Scriptures decisively shaped and resourced the early Christians' understanding of Jesus and of the church. They did that in an imaginative and intuitive rather than an analytic and systematic fashion. Matthew wants to understand the surprising story of Jesus' birth and early life, and does so by putting a verse of the Scriptures alongside incidents within it that gives him and his community some insight regarding what on earth that was about and what it meant (Matt 1.18–2.23). Paul wants to provide a rationale for the material support of apostles or to shake a congregation into living more uprightly or to underline how Jesus must reign over everything, and one of the ways he does so is by incorporating passages from the Scriptures into his argument (1 Cor 9.9; 10.1–13; 15.27). There are some implicit theological principles that underlie this use of Scripture, such as the fact that the Scriptures are the Spirit-inspired words of God to Israel, that Jesus is the climax of Israel's story, and that a Christian congregation is a local embodiment of what Israel was called to be. But there are no exegetical principles involved in it. Matthew and Paul are interested in how the Spirit who inspired the Scriptures is using them to speak to the questions that concern their later readers. To discover this, they do not try to work out by rational means what the Scriptures signified in their historical context in the light of what their authors were seeking to communicate to their audiences, so that they can then infer from that what they might have to say in another context. They intuit how this is happening. One of the symbols of that is the serendipitous way in which they quote from the text, sometimes translating straightforwardly from the Hebrew, sometimes quoting the Septuagint's Greek translation, sometimes adapting the text to make it correspond more precisely to what they have heard the Holy Spirit saying now.

There are implicit theological principles involved in it, but no exegetical principles

The strength of pre-modern interpretation is its capacity to generate powerful application of Scripture that speaks directly to new contexts, addressing questions that arise there. The understanding of Jesus and of the church that we derive from the New Testament could not have existed without the resource of the Old Testament Scriptures, which mediated key insights to the New Testament writers. Indeed, they did this for Jesus himself. At his baptism his Father addressed him in words that come from Psalm 2, Genesis 22, and Isaiah 42, *You are my son, my beloved, with whom I am well-pleased*. These words set before him crucial insights on his identity and vocation.

Modern Interpretation

Modern interpretation came into existence in the West through the collocation of the Renaissance, the Reformation, and the Enlightenment. The Renaissance gave birth to an interest in the human side of texts from the past and to a desire to understand them in their own right. The Reformation brought into focus the problem of conflicts of interpretation—what happens when people disagree on the meaning of texts, as Catholics, Protestants, and Anabaptists did? The Enlightenment led to a realization that there was a difference between the biblical story and both the history of Israel and the 'historical Jesus.' Because of its commitment to history, it assumed we should abandon the biblical story for the history that lay behind it. Further, biblical criticism declined to be bound by the church's tradition regarding the meaning of Scripture, whether it was more catholic or more protestant/evangelical tradition.

The strengths and weaknesses of modern interpretation formed a mirror-image of those of pre-modern. In theory it opened up new possibilities of entering into what was going on between (say) Jeremiah and God and of escaping from the interpretations of the Christian tradition that had overlaid God's word, especially in the Old Testament. In practice it led interpreters into a marsh of critical study, in which they wandered round in circles unable to find any firm footing and forgetting why they had ventured there, and from which they never returned. A century or two's countless dull biblical commentaries witness to this sad story.

The marsh consumed evangelicals as well as liberals

An ironic aspect of this story is the way the marsh consumed evangelicals as well as liberals. Evangelical commentaries were also dull and predictable, but in different ways from liberal commentaries, largely confining themselves to paraphrasing the text and reassuring their readers that the events were historical, really. They were a world away from the dynamic of Calvin, who like Ignatius had the good sense to live after the Renaissance but before the Enlightenment.

Another ironic aspect to the story is the way evangelical scholars tried to come to terms with the nature of pre-modern interpretation, especially as represented by the New Testament. They had a number of strategies. Either the New Testament usage was exegetically sound after all. And/or there were theological principles behind its usage that made its moves acceptable—the use of Hosea 11 in Matthew 2 was justified because it presupposed a typological relationship between Jesus and Israel (this might be true, but it is a modern explanation, not one that underlies Matthew's own thinking). And/or the New Testament generated its exegesis by first-century methods, but we can produce the same results by means of modern exegesis. And/or its acceptance of non-historical exegesis parallels its acceptance of slavery: it was a necessary condescension to its age, but the historical nature of the gospel means that historical exegesis is a fruit of the gospel, like emancipation.

When I myself expounded theories like these, I was sidestepping an uneasy conscience. I knew that pre-modern exegesis was alive and well in my own experience from time to time. God sometimes spoke to me by making Scripture signify something different from what it 'really' meant. God had no need to do that; it would have been quite possible to direct my mind to some passage of

Scripture that actually said what God wanted me to hear, or to give someone else a message from God for me. Instead of that, God chose to use Scripture in a pre-modern way. For God and for us these texts that have become 'Scripture' have thereby gained an importance that makes God inclined to use their words in ways that need not correspond to their original meaning.

Postmodern Interpretation

The nature of postmodern interpretation is to try to move beyond the antitheses of pre-modern and modern. As is often the case, each was right and strong in what it affirmed but wrong and weak in what it (implicitly or explicitly) denied. Or we could look in deconstructionist fashion for the points at which each was implicitly granting what it explicitly denied. For instance, modern interpretation aimed at objectivity in interpretation. It wanted to discover what the text referred to historically. But its priorities and methods were thus different from those of the scriptural text. In absolutizing the importance of history, it brought its subjective priorities and aims to the text, and ignored other aspects of the text that it claimed to be seeking to interpret. The text was concerned with questions about God, truth and life, but modern study systematically bracketed out these questions. The nearest it would get was to consider matters such as faith, ethics, and spirituality, questions about what human beings believed or did rather than what was true or right. Indeed, modern study would rarely even reach these matters. Either way, modern interpretation failed to live up to its own professed concern to do justice to the texts' own agenda.

This is not to imply that we should revert to pre-modern interpretation. The problems that modern interpretation sought to handle were not imaginary. I find it to be more the case in the USA than in Britain that students come to study Scripture with a framework of beliefs that derive more from evangelical tradition than from Scripture, concerning matters such as creation, the fall and sin, divine omniscience and omnipotence, the impossibility of God's having a change of mind, the significance of prayer and the nature of worship, the nature of the atonement, and the necessity of scriptural historicity and inerrancy. Studying Scripture in a modern way is thus really important. We need to distance ourselves from Scripture as we are familiar with it so as to let it say what it has to say in its own terms. Our present understanding is probably wrong at some points and we need delivering from our framework of interpretation. We need to understand Scripture historically.

A framework of beliefs that derives more from evangelical tradition than from Scripture

But we also need to recapture the power of pre-modern interpretation, which focuses more on the question 'What does this signify for *me*?'—or rather 'for *us*?' For the pre-modern assumption is that Scripture belongs to the Christian community and that the natural place to study it is the company of other people. So we ask, how does Scripture address questions that are important for us? How does it bring to the surface issues that we are not quite facing? How does it bring good news regarding the anxieties we do not face because if there is no good news, we dare not do so? How does studying it in the company of other people enable me to see things there that I would otherwise miss, or rescue me from misperceptions that arise from my personal agenda?

The Value of Ignatian Reading

Modern interpretation assumed that in principle texts were always of univocal meaning. If we had enough information, we could discover what they meant. And generally that assumption proves fruitful. But it is not always so. Sometimes it does not seem that the information available to us is ever going to generate an agreed interpretation. Whether this is because we lack the necessary information or because the text has more than one meaning, pre-modern interpretation is happy with not being sure which meaning of the text is correct, because it can work profitably with the process of looking at texts with several possible meanings, asking what happens when I look at this text in the light of these.

Modern interpretation assumed that textual interpretation is an affair of the mind and it can give only a formal place to the Holy Spirit's activity in the interpretation of Scripture. Ignatian interpretation assumes there are mysteries about our understanding of ourselves and our understanding of God that take more than intellectual resolving. The Holy Spirit uses Scripture to penetrate through our blindness to enable us to see ourselves before God. We can then think in linear fashion about such shafts of insight—in fact, we are wise to do so, as part of the process of discerning whether they are indeed shafts of insight. But the insight comes more intuitively and imaginatively than linearly. Ignatian interpretation thus complements more rational, linear, objective, distancing forms of biblical study.

Ignatian interpretation assumes God speaks to people directly through Scripture

Modern interpretation assumed that biblical narrative was history, with the high boredom potential of that designation. Ignatian interpretation assumes that biblical narrative is story—not that it did not happen, but that we need to enter into it as story, into the lives of the characters and the unfolding of the scene, and find our own place there.

Modern interpretation replaced the authority of the church and its tradition with the authority of scholars. For personal Bible study, people then needed commentaries or Bible study notes written by experts, which mediated between Scripture and people. Ignatian interpretation assumes that God speaks to people directly through the words of Scripture. A wise pastor or a group of Christians provide the safeguards and stimulus that other written material might provide.

2

It is a natural human instinct to look back and to look forward.

We do it on annual occasions and special occasions, when we meet friends or family we have not seen for a while and when we give our testimony. We do it on a more everyday basis and as we daydream and when me meet family or friends for dinner ('How has your day been?,' 'What have you got to do tomorrow?'). We do it as we lie in bed waiting to drop off to sleep, recalling events of the day and thinking about what will happen next day. We do it while we sleep, and wake refreshed because we have continued to enjoy the fruitfulness of good things, or wake with a headache because subconsciously we have been processing tricky events or worrying about what we have to face tomorrow.

Job undertakes a comprehensive review of his life in the midst of a terrible experience in middle age

In the Bible people look back and look forward in this way. Deuteronomy 26.1–11 provides Israel with a ceremonial way of doing it each year. They bring some of their harvest to the sanctuary and give their testimony. They recall how their ancestors had been landless wanderers and then an oppressed ethnic minority, but became a great nation. They had cried out to God in their suffering and God had delivered them from it, bringing them into a fruitful land of their own. Now they are in a position to express their gratefulness to God by bringing some of the land's fruit. After giving their testimony, they join in a great celebration embracing the family and people in their midst who have no family.

In Job 29–31, Job undertakes a comprehensive review of his life in the midst of a terrible experience in middle age. His life fell apart through a series of calamities, and he has listened to his counsellors offering him chapter after chapter of implausible interpretation of what has been happening. One of his great strengths is his insistence on facing facts. First he recalls how things used to be—God related to him like a friend, his family was intact, he had people's respect, he was in a position to support the needy and stand up to the oppressor. Then he describes how things are—God has abandoned him and does not respond to his cries, he lives in physical affliction and inner turmoil, and people despise him. Third, he reviews his moral life and declares that he cannot see great sin— in his sex life, his business, his marriage, his family, his concern about the poor, his attitude to money, or his stance in relation to people who do not like him.

In Ecclesiastes 1–2, the author imagines a 'son of David,' presumably Solomon, thinking back over his life. Jewish tradition envisages Solomon doing this in old age, though it would be nice to think of him gaining these insights before that! He reviews the learning he has gained, the ways he has enjoyed himself, the things he has achieved, the 'stuff' he has acquired, and the work he has given himself to. He now realizes that all this constituted busy-ness without ultimate meaning—especially because it will all end in death. He needs to get a more balanced view of life that finds enjoyment in food, work, and insight as gifts of God, but does not pretend they are more than they actually are.

In Philippians 3, Paul thinks back over his life and looks into the future. He too recalls the things he used to value—his position as a member of the Jewish people, his dedication to God as a Pharisee, his commitment to shaping his life by Scripture. As a result of Jesus' confronting him on the Damascus road, he has come to see that these are actually worthless compared with the relationship with God he has entered through meeting Christ. His aim now is to know Christ and the power of his resurrection. It is to share his sufferings so that he may also attain a resurrection like his.

2 Timothy 4 offers another review of Paul's life, set near its end. He is in the midst of being poured out to God as a drink offering. Looking back, he can say that he has fought a good fight, finished his race, kept the faith. Looking forward, he pictures God awarding him his 'gold' when he crosses the finishing line and climbs the victory podium.

What Reviewing Does

From these examples of a review process in Scripture a number of features emerge. It is our reflection on our own experience—we look for the way God is involved in that. It is something that communities and individuals do. It involves thinking, symbolic acts, and putting our reflection into words for others. It recognizes that our lives combine tough experiences and joyful ones, in varying configurations—some people have difficulty owning the joyful ones, some owning the tough ones. It recognizes that we may not be good at interpreting our experience; for years Ecclesiastes and Paul lived by a set of assumptions they eventually realized were wrong. There are times when we may be tempted to forget about joyful experiences, and Israel needed occasions to commemorate what God

The review process recognizes that we may not be good at interpreting our experience

had done for them in the past and in the present, partly so that these then shaped their attitude to life and to God. There are times when we may be tempted to stop owning the good things we have done—Job's friends wanted him to see himself as a moral failure when he was not, and many people have internalized

Job's friends. It is tough recognizing unpleasant truth, but we can do that in the company of the God who gives life (so Ecclesiastes). Sometimes we have to recognize that what we thought were positive aspects of our life were actually negative ones or to see the potential fruitfulness in what we thought were unfruitful aspects. Insight may come when we reconsider our lives in the light of Jesus' resurrection, Jesus' dying, and our resurrection (so Paul).

Job's friends wanted him to see himself as a moral failure when he was not

Ignatius also encouraged a process of *daily* review, which he called the 'examen.' The reworking that follows uses insights from scriptural examples of people looking backward and forward, and other insights from human experience and Christian tradition, to develop a pattern of daily or weekly or periodic review. If you do not know how to pray, it helps you to find a way into prayer—indeed, in a sense it *is* prayer, if you are doing it in dialogue with God. You are talking through the day with God as you might do that with a friend or your spouse. It may give you things to thank God for, to apologize to God for, and to ask for help with. It helps you to 'process' the day— to bring some mental and emotional and spiritual closure to what has been happening.

That is the theory, but I myself can think I have processed the day with God but next morning wake with that headache that signifies I have been doing this overnight, and I have to work out what that was all about! You have to discover the feelings and concerns *underneath* your immediate reactions to the day—the joys and the pains you find it hard to acknowledge. This is one advantage of doing the review with others—they may know the questions to ask to help you do that. Here is a way of doing a daily review.

- Quieten yourself—focus—centre. A biblical symbol to focus on may be helpful (a picture of a rainbow or a tree, bread, water, wine, a palm cross, some silk to represent Jesus' empty grave clothes, an icon, a candle…). Or you may be able to look through a window at something that has symbolic significance.

- Think back over the day—things that happened, things you did, conversations you had.

- As you recollect them, what makes you smile? What makes you grimace? What are you grateful for? What are you ungrateful for? What are you proud of? What are you ashamed of?

- Think about the fact that Jesus is sitting with you. Listen for what he says when you tell him your answers to those questions.

Over a period of time you may reflect on the following questions:

- The things that make you smile in gratitude are life-giving aspects of your experience. Is there some pattern to these? Does Jesus encourage you to make sure there are more of these in your life?

- Or does he want you not to overvalue them? Are there ways in which the life-giving could become life-constraining?

- The things that make you grimace are life-draining aspects of your experience. Is there some pattern to those? Does Jesus encourage you to rework your life to reduce these?

- Or are there ways in which you need to look for the resourcing that will help you keep living with them, so that they are not life-draining?

- The things that make you proud may be clues to the particular gifts or strengths God has given you. Is there some pattern to these? Does that point to some aspect of God's calling?

- The things that make you ashamed point to particular weaknesses. Are there ways in which you are in special danger here, or ways in which you need to seek new help or to set up safeguards?

- What does all this tell you about God's vision for you?

Here are two of my own experiences in doing this review. Once I was finding I could not make myself do it. I had been thinking about some theological uneases I had about the form of the Ignatian scheme we were using, but I knew this was probably a rationalization. There was something I was avoiding. I acknowledged this to my group, and next morning I knew what the problem was. My whole work life had been out of routine for several weeks and subconsciously I was not liking my days *at all*. So I did not want to review them. As it happened, that realization coincided with the arrival of a time when I could get my life in order again.

I acknowledged it to my group, and the next morning I knew what the problem was

Once I was feeling the stress of my job and I told God that I needed to get out of it into something with less responsibility. God said 'Tough, but I will be with you.' And God was. That happened again a year or so later. After another year I said it again, and this time I was able to use the argument that from the job's point of view, it was time for someone else to do it. This time God gave me permission to resign the job.

3 The Ignatian Exercises: Reading Scripture

Ignatius' scheme was designed for use on a four-week retreat and for this purpose divides into four weeks covering sin, Christ's birth and ministry, his passion, and his resurrection.

But Ignatius emphasized the need to be flexible about how long one spent on each 'week' or part, and in Ignatian contexts 'week' is a kind of technical term—it does not mean 'week' in the usual chronological sense.

Ignatius also allowed for the possibility of people completing the exercises over an extended period in the context of their ordinary lives, and the scheme in this booklet is designed for that. I was originally introduced to the Exercises through Joseph A Tetlow's handbook to directing people undertaking the Exercises in this way, *Choosing Christ in the World* (St Louis: Institute of Jesuit Sources, 1989). For Ignatius, the Exercises were designed to be undertaken under the guidance of a spiritual director who would adapt them to the needs of the individual. You can incorporate the element of direction in your study by getting a group of four or five people to follow the scheme with you and meet weekly for an hour or two to share and pray. Partly to fit group use, the scheme in this booklet is much more schematic than anything Ignatius envisaged. If you do not have a group, ask a minister to meet weekly for an hour with you to help you talk through what you are seeing and what is happening in this process. It will not matter whether the minister knows the Exercises, only whether he or she is a person of some discernment.

You can incorporate the element of direction in your study by meeting weekly to share and pray

The scheme involves you spending an hour every day for thirty weeks. And in this booklet, from now on 'week' means 'week'!

- Work out where you are going to find the hour you need. Be realistic. You cannot simply add an hour to your day—you need to ask what this will replace.

- It is up to you when you have this hour. The traditional time is first thing in the morning, and this is the only time that works for me—I never manage the change of focus when I need to disengage from the business of the day. But your circumstances and personality may be different and there is nothing sacred about the question of time.

- If you have to miss a day, do not play 'catch-up.' Quality time not coverage is what counts.

- Last thing at night, have a first look at the passage you will be studying the next day, so that your spirit or unconscious starts working on it overnight. Or if you do your main reading later in the day, look through the passage at the beginning of the day.

- Find a place. Have with you your Bible, your journal and pen, your coffee, and a piece of scrap paper. Turn off the phone. At any stage, if you think of things you must remember to do, make a note of them on your scrap paper so you can then put them out of mind.

- Settle yourself and focus, in the way you do when reviewing the day. Remember that God is with you—for example, sitting on the sofa opposite you. Open yourself to God—you might want physically to open your hands and arms, and thus yourself. Ask God to enable you to see and feel things and to respond to them.

- Start reading the passage slowly. Mouth the words. Put the feelings into them. Do it slowly.

- If the passage is a story, enter into it as a story. Use your imagination to recreate the scene. Put yourself in the position of one or another or all of the characters and imagine what is happening for them and what they are saying. And/or eventually insert yourself into the scene and do what you want to do, or imagine what you would feel, or say what you want to say to God or to Jesus or to other characters, and listen for what you hear back.

- Stop as soon as something strikes you—as soon as you feel something. You may sense something encouraging, or some puzzlement, frustration, or anxiety. This may be just a word that resonates with you and pierces into you for reasons you may not immediately know. Do not worry if this is when you are only in line three of the reading.

- Shut your eyes and explore the feeling. Ask what is going on in you. Stay with that for as long as it takes. If you never get back to the passage, that is fine.

- Ignatius uses the terms 'consolation' and 'desolation' to refer to experiences that may come to us through this process. Consolation denotes a positive awareness such as being loved or loving or joyful.

Desolation denotes the more negative-seeming awareness of darkness, turmoil, restlessness, hopelessness, loss of love, tepidness or sadness. The latter may put us on the track of something very important or may refine or test us, so they are positive experiences in disguise.

- If you do get back to the passage, that is also fine. Continue working through it in this way. You may give forty minutes to this process.

- Remember that feeling nothing is one of the things that can go on—and it is not actually a nothing. It may be a signal to what is going on. One or two of my especially significant realizations have come through times when I felt nothing or could not get started.

- You may find that other things strike you. There may be verses you find difficult to understand or interesting theological questions. If so, make a quick note in your journal or on your scrap pad so you can think about these matters later, but do not get preoccupied with them now. Do not turn this reading into a 'head' thing.

- You may find there are aspects of the text that you find objectionable. These may again be theological or ethical questions that you could make a note of and think about later. But in the meantime, ask what your reaction is saying about you. Why do you react the way you do? What issues is it raising within you? What might it mean God wants you to face within yourself?

- When you have finished reading, or are out of time, make notes in your journal of what has been happening and what you have been seeing.

- Talk to God about what has been happening—joys, griefs, praises, resentments, promises…Pray for the other members of your group. Say a psalm or the Lord's Prayer slowly.

- Remember that Ignatius saw the Exercises as a way of discerning whether a person's life needed to take a new direction. Keep an eye on hints of this kind as the weeks go by.

Old Testament Spirituality

Ignatius plausibly assumed that there is a telling sequence in the life of Christ, in the movement from beginnings, to commissioning, to the exercise of a ministry, to suffering and death, to resurrection.

There is an analogous narrative shape to the life of Israel, a movement from promise to deliverance to covenant to possession to faithlessness to loss to renewal. For use by a church, one might shape an Old Testament scheme around that outline of the story of Israel, but for use by individuals I have shaped the present scheme round the Psalms. They make more reference to the lives of ordinary individuals and thus seem a natural starting point for understanding Old Testament spirituality. They provide our framework for reading more broadly in the Old Testament.

The Psalms make more reference to the lives of ordinary people and seem a natural starting point

Form critics often distinguish between three main types of psalm—hymns, laments, and thanksgivings. Hymns simply praise God as holy, faithful, and merciful, as the world's creator and Israel's deliverer, and so on. Laments complain at God, grieve at the fact that God is not behaving in that way in our current experience, and press God to do so again. They are the equivalent to what we call prayer and (when used on behalf of others) intercession, though they are a lot livelier. Thanksgivings are testimonies to God's having answered such prayers—we have seen God act and can now rejoice in what God has done for us. While hymns give praise for who God always is, thanksgivings give praise for what God has just done for us personally in our experience. As Anne Lamott says, 'Here are the two best prayers I know: "Help me, help me, help me," and "Thank you, thank you, thank you."'[1] Form criticism also recognized that while most psalms speak from us to God, there are some

Laments are the equivalent to what we call prayer—though a lot livelier

---

1 *Travelling Mercies* (New York: Pantheon, 1999) p 82. She adds, 'A woman I know says, for her morning prayer, "Whatever," and then for the evening, "Oh, well,"' which encapsulates daily review.

that speak from God to us, more like prophecy—and like prophecy they may either make promises to us or issue challenges to us.

Half the Psalter is laments, and that in itself suggests we need to ask whether this group needs subdividing. I have separated laments into three types. There are ones that do cry 'Help, help, help' out of a sense of abandonment and urgent need. There are others that imply less of a state of panic and more sense of trust. And there are prayers that acknowledge some responsibility for the trouble they describe and thus instead of accusing God of abandoning us, acknowledge that we have abandoned God.

So here are six types of psalm suggesting a six-fold movement between us and God:

Hymns: we declare our conviction about who God is and who we are.

Laments: we own that this has not been working out in experience.

Psalms of trust: we declare that we maintain our confidence in God under pressure.

Confessions: we acknowledge our failure.

Thanksgivings: we testify to what God has done for us personally.

Challenges: we commit ourselves to walk in God's way.

The regular life of faith keeps taking us through this sequence, with greater depth throughout our lives. We keep going deeper in conviction, deeper in owning loss and anger, deeper in maintaining hope, deeper in recognizing our sinfulness, deeper in our appreciation for what God does for us personally, and deeper in our commitment to walking faithfully with God. Given that the Psalter is *the* Old Testament manual for spirituality—indeed, the *biblical* manual for spirituality—that outline ought to have potential for understanding the spirituality of the Old Testament as a whole. So this Old Testament reading scheme gives five weeks for each of the six movements of prayer. The first week in each set focuses on one of the groups of psalms. The succeeding four weeks in each set look at parts of the Old Testament that link with that movement of prayer.

The regular life of faith keeps taking us through this sequence, with greater depth throughout our lives

An Old Testament Reading Scheme   5

Sometimes it is up to you to divide up the material for the week— do it at your own pace according to the way things strike you as you read.

Use the last day each week to revisit the readings that were especially creative or that did not work. For Ignatian spirituality, repetition is a key idea. Sometimes you may see something particularly important in a passage—maybe encouraging, maybe uncomfortable. Go back to that passage and dig deeper. Or you may get nowhere with a passage, and that may be a sign that there is something important here that you are resisting seeing. Once again, go back and see if you can let it reach you.

Because Ignatius' own scheme follows the life of Christ, like the church's year, it is possible to link it with observance of the church's year. Beginning in the autumn, you come to Jesus' birth at Christmas and his death and resurrection at Easter. If you want to take note of the church's year in following the Old Testament scheme, you can add these extra weeks of study.

> *Christmas:* Isaiah 7.1–17; 9.1–7; 11.1–10; 32.1–8; 40.1–11; 42.1–9; 49.1–13
>
> *Holy Week:* Lamentations 1; 2; 3; 4; 5; Psalms 23; 96
>
> *Pentecost:* 1 Samuel 11; Isaiah 30.18–26; 61; 63.7–19; Ezekiel 37.1–14; Joel 2.15–29; Zechariah 4

1 Knowing Who God Is and Knowing Who We Are

Week 1—Psalms of Praise

| Psalm 8 |
| Psalm 19 |
| Psalm 33 |
| Psalm 66 |
| Psalm 96 |
| Psalm 100 |

I have noted that Ignatius prefaced the study of Jesus' life with some meditation on our sin that functions to open us up to our need of Christ. Joseph Tetlow prefaced that with preparatory material encouraging us to trust in God's love and mercy so we can face up to our sin. This led him to an arrangement that also follows the dynamic of Old Testament spirituality as I have outlined it, beginning from convictions about who God is and who we are. In due course we have tough things to face up to. But first, we need to know who God is, how God relates to us, and who we are designed to be.

Through the week, fill out your picture of who God is—maybe have one page in your journal for accumulating this picture through the week—and at the end, ask which elements in the picture are especially significant for you, and why. In a parallel way, fill out your picture of who we are, maybe on another page, and at the end ask the same question.

Remember that these psalms are expressions of worship, and take up their repeated invitations to join in the worship of this God. Make each day's reading an extended time of worship as you keep working through the psalm. Keep your eye open for phrases that leap off the page for you. Mine was 'Sing a *new* song'—because at the time I was dwelling on some happy and some bad things from the past. God was telling me to look for what God was doing now and respond to that.

At the beginning and/or end of your meditation each day through the subsequent four weeks, use one of these psalms to worship God—or use other examples of praise psalms: Psalms 29, 47, 48, 65, 68, 78, 87, 93, 95, 97, 98, 99, 104, 105, 111, 113, 114, 117, 122, 134, 135, 145, 146, 147, 148, 149, 150.

Week 2—God As Creator and Us As God's Created

Genesis 1–2

Work through these two creation stories in your own way at your own pace through the week. You could fill in two more pages on who God is and who we are.

The two stories work in different ways and have different focuses. In the first, I found myself fixing on particular ideas and motifs and thinking about those and why they had leapt off the page for me—such as God's turning what was empty or stormy into what was formed and beautiful, and God's introducing light into darkness. In the second, I found myself spending more time imagining the scene (for example, God as the potter shaping a figure out of clay and breathing life into it so that—poof!—it becomes a living man) and wondering at it—that is what God did in creating me!

At the end of your meditation, spend five minutes worshipping by means of one of the psalms from last week's list.

Week 3—How Life is Designed to Work

Prov 8.1–4, 22–36
Prov 3.1–18
Prov 3.19–35
Prov 15
Prov 16
Prov 21

Proverbs 1–9 mostly comprises sermonettes, Proverbs 10–31 mostly one-verse sayings. The material again starts from the way God has created the world and what living in accordance with creation is like. Chapters 10–31 have the advantage that you do not have to read a whole chapter to get some self-contained insight. So read until a verse strikes you, and stay there as long as you need, then move on until another strikes you. Do not worry about getting to the end.

People sometimes find Proverbs annoying because its description of life does not correspond to the way things turn out in experience. It is too simple. It is indeed describing how things are designed to work, not how they necessarily do, and how they generally work, not how they invariably do. Whenever you react to the reading with a theological question like that, make a note and think about the theological question later, but during your meditation make this the way into discovering what is in your own heart. What is it about your own experience or fears or disappointments or anxieties that this passage is hooking? Own that before God and talk to God about it. Then go back to the passage and see what God wants to do with you through it.

Week 4—How We Are Designed to Seek and to Love

Song of Songs offers us further aspects of God's vision for our human lives. Karl Barth described the Song as an extended commentary on Genesis 2.18–25. Admittedly the Song is less of an idyll than that might imply. Social convention disapproves of this couple's love, perhaps because they are not yet betrothed. They themselves are fearful and hesitant as well as longing and enthusiastic in relation to each other. 'Everybody's longing for intimacy… Everybody's fearing for intimacy,' the Irish group *The Corrs* sing.

Unless you have just fallen in love or just married, reading the Song may be a tough experience—especially if you are disappointed in love, or have been abused, or have a failed marriage, or have some other experience that makes love hard to think about. The Song dramatizes the possibility that our own experience may not be all that there is to say about the subject. It invites us to continue believing that God has a vision for relationships with the opposite sex, even when (especially when) it seems unlikely that this vision can be realized for us in the obvious way. It invites us to continue believing in intimacy and to keep enjoying the good things of God's material creation (wine, food, perfume, nature).

Admittedly, as poetry it works in a much more mysterious way than a romantic comedy—think *Sleepless in Seattle* crossed with *Mulholland Drive*. Do not worry that many of the details seem puzzling (commentators find them puzzling, too). The Song is dreamlike and needs entering into like the account of a dream, in a nonlinear, stream-of-consciousness way.

There is a long Christian tradition of allegorizing the Song as a picture of our relationship with God rather than with another human being. If you read it that way, do so with caution, because you could end up with a weird and worrying understanding of God. For instance, God is not like a beloved whom you are not sure you will be able to find. But perhaps God, too, is someone whose intimacy we both want and fear.

Week 5—How God Delivered a People

Exodus 1.1–21
Exodus 1.22–2.22
Exodus 2.23–3.22
Exodus 4.1–31
Exodus 5.1–6.1
Exodus 14.1–31

Israel's own awareness of God was thus shaped by creation, but also by its experience of God's deliverance from Egypt. Exodus includes stories of God's using ordinary individuals in ordinary ways, using an ordinary individual in an extraordinary way, and delivering the people as a whole. These are stories about real life situations that we may be able to imagine our way into; see how you identify with different people in them. How did God interact in different ways with these different people? How do these stories inform or shape your own relationship with God?

2 Owning The Negatives (Hurt, Lost-ness, Grief, Anger...)

Week 6—Psalms that Tell It Like It Is

Psalm 22
Psalm 42–43
Psalm 80
Psalm 85
Psalm 88
Psalm 126

When we know something of who God is, how God acts, and what God's vision is for us, that may give us the confidence to face the negatives in our lives. Or when we know who God is supposed to be, how God is supposed to act, and what God's vision for us is supposed to be, that may give us the impetus to be direct with God about the negatives in our lives. Admittedly these distinctions resist being drawn in a neat way. In reading Psalms or Proverbs or the Song of Songs you may have already protested 'But it is not like that,' and in Exodus we have listened to Israel saying the same thing. In the next five weeks' reading, this becomes the dominant note, though the readings reinforce their invitation to own those negatives by reminding God and reminding us of the facts about God, which make this owning possible and necessary.

The biggest single group of psalms comprises ones starting from a situation where the statements about God in the psalms of praise do not work out. In reaction to that experience, they express a range of emotions, such as anger, abandonment, depression, fear, and isolation. And they express a range of ways of relating to those statements about God, such as simply abandoning them, or struggling to hold onto them, or hoping for them to be true again in the future. They do that on behalf of ordinary individuals, or individuals in a leadership position, or communities going through tough experiences. One way or another they therefore invite us to acknowledge our own such experiences before God, and to press God to do something about them. In these prayers we do not blame ourselves for what has gone wrong in our lives (we have a chance to do that later!). These prayers arise out of hurt or loss that we cannot see is our fault, and invite us to challenge God about what has happened.

At the beginning and/or end of your meditation each day through the subsequent four weeks, use one of these psalms to lay hold on God, or use other examples of such psalms. Here is a categorization of these—it is sometimes uncertain, so do not worry if you are puzzled as to why I have put particular examples where I have.

For an individual: Psalms 6, 10, 26, 31, 38, 39, 40, 54, 55, 56, 57, 58, 59, 64, 70, 71, 86, 109, 120, 141, 142

For a leader: Psalms 3, 5, 7, 13, 17, 25, 28, 35, 61, 63, 69, 102, 140, 143

For a congregation: Psalms 12, 44, 60, 74, 79, 83, 89, 90, 94, 106, 123, 137, 144

Week 7—Owning Meaninglessness

Ecclesiastes

We think that doing things, discovering things, enjoying ourselves, achieving things, buying things, or going to new places can make our lives meaningful. As Christians we put a religious gloss on all this (we are doing things for God or going to new places for God) but the dynamic is the same. The genius of Ecclesiastes is to invite us to face the fact that none of this can ever work. Whether we can face that partly depends on whether we have something else to put in its place—for example the truths we studied in weeks 1–5. Ecclesiastes does not go on totally to dismiss enjoyment, achievement, wisdom, and so on. It affirms them as God's gifts. They become pernicious when treated as if they had ultimate meaning, but when we see them as having a much more limited significance, we can enjoy them as God's gifts. They are not everything but they are not nothing. They are not enough, but they are not nothing.

Week 8—Owning Abandonment

Job 1–2
Job 3
Job 6
Job 7
Job 14
Job 23

Job is about the 'problem of suffering,' but it does not attempt to 'solve' the problem—suffering is not the kind of problem that can be solved. The deepest pain about Job's suffering is his experience of abandonment. The opening tells us how God came to allow that. But Job never knows about these reasons, which means he has to live through his experience of abandonment the same way as we often do. After the opening, the suggested chapters are some of the ways Job talks to God in his abandonment. We can put ourselves into his position and make his protests our own—to see what we might mean if we spoke to God like this.

If you want to know more about his story, Job 38–42 tells of God's eventual appearing to Job (still not telling him about Job 1–2) and eventually restoring him.

Week 9—Owning Disappointment and Fear (and Dealing with it in People)

Numbers 11–14
Numbers 20

Paul urges one of his churches to learn from these stories about the people on the journey from Sinai to Canaan (see 1 Cor 10), implying we should read them as concerning the people as a group. That reminds us that the point about the Old Testament is often to pull us out of our individualism. We tend to focus on God's relating to us as individuals, but congregations and communities also have lives. They experience birth, maturity, adversity, failure, sin, senescence, and death. God relates to groups as well as to individuals. A strength and a limitation of Ignatian meditation is that it focuses on the individual. In reading these stories, you could imagine the people in the stories as your congregation, as Paul does, and think about yourself as part of that congregation/people.

But you can also identify with Moses, Aaron, and Miriam, with the pressures the people put on them, the way they cope (or do not cope) with these, and the toughness of the way they get treated.

Week 10—When God is Tough

1 Samuel 13
1 Samuel 15
1 Samuel 28
2 Samuel 6
2 Samuel 11–12
2 Samuel 24

These are among the hardest stories in the Bible, so it would be a great loss if they were not there. Their genius is to represent within Scripture the reality of how life sometimes is— grossly unfair. The Old Testament does not attribute this merely to human sin or demonic deception, which leaves God safely out of control of the world. It describes God as creator of disaster as well as well-being, former of darkness as well as light (Isaiah 45.7). This does not imply God causes every disaster, except for the sense in which God lies behind everything that happens. It does imply that God directly causes some disasters and sometimes behaves in ways that seem overly tough. This is not of course merely an Old Testament conviction (see Acts 5).

Tough events happen to Saul and David because they are leaders of God's people, so this week's readings overlap in their implications with Week 9. Saul and David have the experiences that they do because they are Israel's first and second kings. Ordinary people get away with things that leaders do not, and later kings get away with things that these first two kings do not. David is complicated, because he also gets away with worse deeds than the ones Saul is cast off as king for. Because of their calling, leaders may experience great blessing, but also great toughness. We need to remember, though, that the toughness of God's relating to Saul and both the mercy and the toughness of God's relating to David says nothing about what was going on in their relationship with God. Being cast off as leader does not mean you are cast out of relationship with God.

Week 11—Psalms that Hold onto Trust and Hope

Psalm 16
Psalm 27
Psalm 62
Psalm 84
Psalm 119.41–64
Psalm 139

Intermingled with the psalms that own the negatives are psalms that may also come out of tough situations but are more characterized by a continuing hopefulness. Try to get inside some of the series of powerful images that run through these psalms—refuge, light, stronghold, shelter, rock, fortress, home, sun, shield.

When you get to Psalm 139, do not get stuck at vv 1–18; vv 19–24 are the climax of the psalm. In the light of the fact that God knows all about us and can reach out to us wherever we are, here we express a serious commitment to avoid getting entangled in wickedness. Here we are not asking God to punish people who hate us, but promising to hate people who hate God—in the sense that we totally repudiate their standards.

Over the next four weeks you can continue to use these six psalms as the framework for your prayers, or you can use other instances of psalms that hold onto trust and hope in this way: Psalms 4, 11, 14, 23, 36, 41, 46, 52, 67, 75, 76, 77, 101, 108, 115, 121, 125, 129, 131, 132.

Week 12—Embodying Grace and Commitment

Ruth

The story of Ruth invites us to enter imaginatively into the lives of a series of characters—Elimelech, Naomi, Mahlon and Chilion, Orpah, Ruth, Boaz and David. The three main characters all have their weaknesses or skeletons in their cupboards—Naomi with her bitterness, Ruth as a Moabite (see Numbers 25), Boaz as a descendant of Judah and Tamar (see Genesis 38). In different ways they embody loss and blessing. In different ways they become the means of mediating God's love to one another; note expressions that recur, such as steadfast love or commitment (RSV, NIV 'kindness'), grace or favour, refuge, comfort, and redeemer (the next-of-kin who acts to restore things to what they should be).

Week 13—Being a Man of God: Elisha

2 Kings 2
2 Kings 4.1–17
2 Kings 4.18–44
2 Kings 5
2 Kings 6.1–23
2 Kings 6.24–7.20

Several of the Elisha stories likewise concern ordinary people's everyday experiences, but others are broader in focus. All picture God's involvement in people's lives in spectacular ways, in miraculous healing and miraculous provision—like stories about Jesus. They thus give us opportunity to imagine being in the situations of need that come to the characters and experiencing God provide like that, and to identify needs of ours that might be analogous, or possibilities that lie in God's capacity to be involved with us.

Week 14—Living in the World

Esther *or*
Daniel 1
Daniel 2.1–24
Daniel 3
Daniel 4
Daniel 5
Daniel 6

Do not read both of these! Remember that effective reading often involves not reading more but less, and letting the material do its work on you. If you are a woman you may especially want to read Esther, though perhaps if you are man you may especially gain from reading Esther both for the way God uses women in the story and the way the men react to that and work with it. Read Esther at your own pace, stopping to dwell at points that ring bells. If you do get through the story in less than a week, you can then also read one or two of the Daniel stories. Whereas Esther is one complete story, Daniel comprises a series of individual stories that keep revisiting similar issues. Both concern people living outside the promised land, settled in foreign countries, and thus portray God relating to our life in a world that does not acknowledge God.

Week 15—Living with God's Promises: Abraham and Sarah

Genesis 12.1–13.1
Genesis 15
Genesis 16
Genesis 17
Genesis 18
Genesis 22

We are inclined to idealize people such as Abraham and Sarah, but God is involved with them with their strengths and their weaknesses. The stories speak of these weaknesses in matter-of-fact ways as realities that do not put God off from working with and through them. They may free us to own some of our own weaknesses and trust God to work with and through us. The stories also speak matter-of-factly of the pressures on God's promises that come from circumstances and other people and even from God, and they may free us also to own these.

4 Owning Failure (Sin)

Week 16—Psalms of Confession

Psalm 25
Psalm 32
Psalm 38
Psalm 51
Psalm 90
Psalm130

Whereas most 'lament' psalms arise out of situations when things have gone wrong and we cannot see it is our fault, this week's psalms recognize we do need to acknowledge our failures. To judge from the fact that there are only a small number of them, it is worth noting that in the Old Testament people seem less preoccupied by sin than Christians are. Sin is less prominent in the gospels, too. Like the Old Testament, Jesus invited us to be confident about our relationship with God on the basis of God's love for us. God is not put off by our shortcomings

If we lack confidence in God's love, we may not be able properly to face our failures. Thinking about our sin then just makes us feel more guilty without that emotion being able to have positive fruit in motivating us to face our shortcomings in an adult way, with the possibility of then making progress in our commitment. So let this week, and the following weeks, have their proper role in helping you face up to the shortcomings in your life and character in a way that can be creative.

Week 17—The Spheres of Our Sin and the Way it Works

Genesis 3.1–13
Genesis 3.14–24
Genesis 4.1–10
Genesis 4.11–24
Genesis 6.1–4 and
9.20–27
Genesis 11.1–9

Christians separate off Genesis 3 from what follows and treat is as *the* exposition of how sin came into the world. In your reading resist this. Genesis 1–11 as a whole is about how sin came into the world and came to affect the different spheres of life. These stories show sin operating in our relationship with God, our partners, our work, our brothers and sisters, our parents, and our communities. It brings out into the open spheres of sin that we avoid talking about, such as sexual abuse.

The story that follows on from Genesis 1–11 concerns historical events, and I presume that this is true of Genesis 1–11 itself. But this story is expressed in metaphors and pictures; I do not know what the camcorder would have caught. Further, while it is talking about events that happened once-for-all, the story also illustrates how sin continues to operate in our lives.

Week 18—How Sin Affects Our Relationship with God

Exodus 32–34

These chapters, too, go back to events that happened in history, yet they are something bigger than that. They offer a series of takes on how God reacts to sin and what God does about it. This is thus not a narrative that works in straightforward linear fashion, like Esther or Ruth. Again, think *Mulholland Drive* or *Vanilla Sky*. Each episode in the story says something concrete about God and sin. Episodes may seem to contradict each other, because a series of truths about God and sin need to be held in tension with each other. For instance, God does forgive, but God does discipline and purify. When an episode seems scandalous, ask why it has that effect on you—or move onto the next!

Week 19—Forms of Sin: Religiousness, Violence, Family Sin, Sexual Sin

Judges 2
Judges 5
Judges 9
Judges 11
Judges 16
Judges 19

Judges includes the most unpleasant stories in Scripture. The book epitomizes God's ruthlessness in requiring us to face the facts about how things are in the world. Be horrified by what you read, but do not shy away from it, because it describes the world we live in, and we may find here things we have done, or things that have been done to us, or things that affect communities or families we know.

Week 20—How We Are Implicated in Our People's Sin

Amos

For members of many nations, including the entire First World, one of our most intractable problems is the way we share responsibility for the wrongdoing in our nation. One aspect of this is our materialism, which Christians usually share with non-Christians, and which links with our oppression of peoples in the Two-Thirds World. Reading Amos made me see myself again as a member of a nation on its way to God's judgment. It pushes me to pray God to have mercy, as Amos does.

Do not worry too much about the historical events referred to, for example in chapters 1–2. In most cases we do not know much more than what Amos actually says, and the kind of events being referred to are clear enough.

5 Rediscovering God's Grace and Power

Week 21—Psalms of Thanksgiving

Psalm 30
Psalm 34
Psalm 73
Psalm 103
Psalm 116
Psalm 138

We come to the last group of psalms that speak from us to God. You can imagine how someone prayed Psalm 80 (for example) a little while ago, then saw God deliver them or heal them or restore them, and in these psalms they come back to give public testimony to what God has done for them. Other thanksgiving psalms are 9, 18, 92, 107, 118, 124, and 136. You could use these to frame your prayers over the next four weeks.

Week 22—How We Never Learn

Genesis 25.19–34
Genesis 27.1–45
Genesis 27.46–28.22
Genesis 32.1–21
Genesis 32.22–32
Genesis 33.1–20

Jacob is a manipulative person. Does he ever change? Christians have usually reckoned that he does, because we like Hollywood endings. I cannot see it myself, even though I also like a Hollywood ending when I can get one. God persists with Jacob even though he remains spiritually half-witted. The sobering but encouraging fact is that Jacob is the person who becomes Israel. As the people of God, we can see ourselves in Jacob-Israel. God does not make much progress with us, but that does not make God cast us off.

You are free to disagree with my reading of his story. The question to concern yourself with is not merely which is the right reading but what is happening to you as you do the reading. What reading appeals to you and what does not, and why, and what is God saying to you through asking those questions?

Week 23—How We Combine Insight and Blindness

Joseph is also a puzzle and an encouragement, though for different reasons. Joseph is a self-aggrandizing, narcissistic person—consider his dreams, or the way he manipulates his brothers, or the way he turns the whole of the Egyptian

Genesis 37	people into state slaves. But he is a gifted leader and adminis-
Genesis 39	trator and is capable of huge faith, huge faithfulness, and huge
Genesis 40	generosity. I cannot put the two sides of the picture together.
Genesis 41	But then, most of us have our own contradictions, so maybe
Genesis 45	Joseph can help us to see them—especially as we see how
Genesis 50	God again seems relaxed about them and works through
	Joseph anyway.

Week 24—How We Can Prove God's Mercy and Faithfulness

2 Chron 6.12–42	2 Chronicles tells the story of the people of Israel. Part-
2 Chron 7.1–22	way through, the nation splits into two, Ephraim and
2 Chron 14.1–15.7	Judah. Ephraim is taken off into exile, but anyway the
2 Chron 20.1–30	book focuses on Judah. The story alternates accounts
2 Chron 32.1–26	of periods of faithlessness with periods of reform when
2 Chron 34.1–33	the people prove God's love, grace, mercy, and power.

These six passages begin with the crucial event of the consecration of the temple and then comprise excerpts from the reigns of some of the kings who led the people in returning to the God of Israel and proving that mercy and faithfulness.

Week 25—How God Encourages the Forsaken

Isaiah 40.1–11	Not long after Josiah's day, the Babylonians destroyed
Isaiah 41.8–20	Jerusalem and took many Judeans into exile in Babylon.
Isaiah 42.1–9	There they had to stay for fifty years till the Babylonian
Isaiah 42.18–43.7	empire itself fell. Isaiah 40–55 comes from late in that
Isaiah 54.1–17	period. The people have become demoralized and have
Isaiah 55.1–13	lost faith. They have no hope that God will ever come
	back to them or restore them. Here God's word is de-
	signed to rebuild their faith and hope.

6 Committing Ourselves to God's service

Week 26—Psalms that Speak from God to Us

Psalm 1	The shape of Old Testament spirituality is the same as that of
Psalm 15	the New—or rather, the New Testament adopts the shape of
Psalm 24	that of the Old, as it would need to do if it was to see itself as a
Psalm 37	fulfilment of the Old. So having seen ourselves as grasped by
Psalm 50	God's grace, we are in a position to make a renewed commit-
Psalm 81	ment to being God's people.

To begin with, then, there is a last group of Psalms, ones that speak from God to us in words of blessing often interwoven with declarations of God's expectations of us. This is no accidental collocation, for the Psalms' promise is that (to put it in Jesus' words), if you first seek God's rule, things such

27

as food, drink, clothing, and long life will be yours as well. As well as the seven psalms listed above, we might include Psalms 2, 14, 20, 21, 45, 49, 53, 72, 82, 91, 110, 112, 127, 128, and 133 in this category.

Week 27—God's Expectations of Us

Deuteronomy 4–11

Psalm 1 blessed people who meditate on the Lord's teaching. That meditation is what we do through this week. Deuteronomy 4–11 comprises a huge rolling repetitive exhortation about the fundamental attitudes God looks for from Israel, which are then spelled out in terms of detailed commitments in the following chapters. Read it at your own pace, stopping to spend time on motifs that seem significant for you.

Week 28—Heeding God's Call

1 Samuel 3
Isaiah 6
Jeremiah 1
Ezekiel 2.3–3.21
Isaiah 61
Nehemiah 1

There is a whole series of accounts in Scripture of how people get called to God's service, mostly of how people came to be prophets. The people of God usually reject prophets, so prophets need a strong sense of God's call and the people need a clear reminder that they are rejecting one God has sent. The language of 'call' waters down the idea, because in Scripture God's call is a peremptory summons that you evade at your peril—see Jonah!

Week 29—Persisting with God's Call

1 Kings 19; Amos 7
Jeremiah 36
Ezekiel 33
Isaiah 49
Nehemiah 4–5

Actually Jonah was wise, because there is a price attached to God's call. We have noted that it is likely to mean rejection, or opposition, or danger. Face the price and ask what it means for you, but also note the encouragements offered by these different testimonies.

Week 30—Being a Servant of God

Deut 31
Deut 32.48–52, 34.1–12
Joshua 1
Joshua 3–4
Joshua 23
Joshua 24

In Scripture, the idea of leadership is an ambiguous one. Leaders as often lead the community astray as they lead them on with God. The category the Old Testament prefers is that of servant—not servant of the people but servant of God. So if you see yourself as a leader, repent and start thinking of yourself as a servant of God, and read the story of the end of Moses' life (we have looked at earlier stages in weeks 5, 9 and 18) and the ministry of Joshua as his successor, and ask what God might be calling you to. At the end of these thirty weeks, look back over the journey you have travelled and see whether there has been any particular direction to it.